All These Things Were Real: Poems of Delerium Tremens

Michelle Reale

West Philly Press
Philadelphia

Cover illustration: "Untitled" by David A. Reale

ISBN: 1545342881

ISBN-13: 9781545342886

WestPhillyPress.com

"But anybody who's never had delirium tremens even in their early stages may not understand that it's not so much a physical pain but a mental anguish indescribable to those ignorant people who don't drink and accuse drinkers of irresponsibility."

— **Jack Kerouac**, *Big Sur*

"Mendacity is a system that we live in," declares Brick. "Liquor is one way out an' death's the other."

— **Tennessee Williams**, *Cat on a Hot Tin Roof*

"The bottle is damned faithful, he said,
the bottle will not lie"
— **Charles Bukowski**, *Play the Piano Drunk Like a Percussion Instrument Until the Fingers Begin to Bleed a Bit*

For D.A.R.

---Speranze vive

de·lir·i·um tre·mens

dəˌlirēəm ˈtremənz/

noun

noun: **delirium tremens**

a psychotic condition typical of withdrawal in chronic alcoholics, involving tremors, hallucinations, anxiety, and disorientation.

Mirabilis

We make ourselves whole with
cadaver bone and cat gut spun

to appropriate resiliency. Weaved
in, out and around soft pink flesh.

It is a year or it is never.

This is limbic revision. It requires a fancy
negotiation of steep curves, headlong into

a point of entry sans fashionable headgear,
padding, or signals of warning. The knowledge

of seasickness, learned in the briny amniotic sac
suppresses the rage against the soft heart

of excessive mothering. I was not groomed
for the role, yet reality was complicit.

You rested your head against pockmarked walls.

You have always had the benefit of first refusal.
Remember the mother who beat her child

on a street in Rome, like a martyr, braying.
The child had no *consapovolezza*[1]; it shook you.

---

[1] "awareness"

I told you: *look away, press your feet*
into ancient paving stones. You sought forgiveness

without reason; I knew that you would.
God forbid one should *experience*. And now?

Don't go. But if you do, don't come back the same way.

Genesis

You opened the refrigerator and I smelled
green grass and lactose. *Out of my way.*
Witness here, the brain
in revolt.

The egg you squeezed in your hand,
a blessing to all beginnings. The blood from
the yolk dripped through

your white-knuckled fist. You were no
longer hungry and the pain in your stomach felt
like a branding iron.

The sheen of sweat on the forehead,
the tenuous grasp on space and time,
twists your foot

into an asteroid of hope. You called it
Vesta. You said: *vestavestavesta,*
and you smiled.

Tribal in your cultural
appropriating, both expressing
and betraying linear

logic. We understand
in our misunderstanding. A black
force is gathering

momentum, and every newspaper
article has the cold hard prose of
tragedy reportage

that I clucked sympathetically
to and then went on to the next
thing, oblivious

Visits my five-chambered heart. I
hold my breath. Say your name
like a benediction

to the afflicted. A momentary
deviation from my hand clutching
the edge of the cliff.

An omen, you would have called it, if only you could.

Rapid Onset

The tall black figures leaned towards him, he could smell.
their fear. Devoid of faces, he asked, *do they expect me
to read their minds?*

The quiver of his chin and a finger up to his
trembling mouth. He is gulping for air, tells
me not to move: A man is playing a Valentine

joke on his wife, we must not interfere! He is
holding his heart in his hand, wrapped in a rusted
chain. She has no idea how much it is worth

but he will tell her. *It's not real,* I repeat, though
I begin to doubt myself. We are bathed in moonlight
and sweat. He looks down at his feet. *You are right.*

It's not real. He loves someone else anyway. I place
my hand on his back, feel the outline of his spine, the
heave of his heavy breathing, a twisted current jolts me.

*Experts warn that when you feel thirsty, you are already
dehydrated.*

Delerium

The dog on the leash
he can manage. A walk

across the yard, the uneven
dirt and he feels his body fold

into itself. *Feed him,* he begs
her. *Take care of him. Please.*

He seats himself at the table. Carefully
places his hands, palm down on the

cool surface.   He looks beyond her, out
the window over the sink.   He sees them

gliding over the grass, their toeless feet
not even touching the grass. They will

wait for him. *Oh, Oh,* she says, fumbles
with the cell phone. *Oh!* Heat travels

the length of her spine, prickles her scalp,
He rubs his eyes, still holding the leash,

the dog entombed in his own confusion, his
own misery. They trade places. He cannot

see out of the window. His hand on his chest
he tells her *this is where fear lives.*

She punches numbers on the phone like a blind
woman with only half a chance.

Advice

At the emergency room, tell them that he aims to harm himself. That you heard it with your own ears. *They will have to admit him.* The first breath you take will be at the mercy of the one you love the most. Don't let it deter you. When he thrashes in the narrow bed, when they forget his name, when the male nurses argue about who's on break next, try not gouge the glibness from their hollow frames. Tug the thin gown over the bare buttocks, the spine contorted, writhing in disintegration. Don't ask for reassurance. There is no word that could comfort. *Let it go.*

Crossing Borders

As irony goes, this is a good one. I
know that what is killing him could

cure him, too. I am on one side of
the divide, he on the other. Something

has forked here. I could wallpaper a house
with receipts for Nikolai Vodka, for Rumpleminz

schnapps, one you can't detect, the other could be
nothing more than assiduous oral hygiene. I want

to place his fragile existence in an ornate curio
in the corner of my favorite room in the house,

safe, unreachable. Is there any leeway to change
the simple format that determines how the road

ahead is paved? His fingernails grow, while everything
else stands still. I mention them to the nurse,

a young woman with her hair in a severe bun,
made up in irritation and sleeplessness.

Least of your worries, she says, one foot across the
threshold and already out the door.

Accusations

The doctor is thin as a lemon slice
concave, holding herself through the middle

as though her skeletal
structure has or will fail her.

Our view is neutral ground, a ten-tiered parking
garage. My son froths a verbal manifesto

against my excessive mothering,
like turning over tables in the temple.

We don't look at each other and
we don't look at him.

I get up to leave, and in an accented voice
she tells me *it's not really him,*

except it sounds like a question.
A whine of the machines and contorted

expressions. She's right--- It *isn't* him.
Not really.

But it isn't me, either.

Unspoken

An arsenal of gold plated medals,
St. Jude, stoic at the top of the heap.
I welcome all the platitudes,
the clucking of the tongues,
the heavy arms around my shoulder,
the *glad-it's-your-son-and-not-mine look.*
He prays to a cracked god with an attitude,
receives the opposite of an answer to prayer
in proportion to absolutely nothing.
What someone else might call
a blessing in disguise, I might call holy
deprivations with a battery acid aftertaste.
My God, the sincerity of them all.

ICU

He fixates on the generic hospital wall art. Three large yellow tulips imprisoned behind a plastic, fake gold frame. *Look,* he says, *they are ovulating!* He'd like to give them his anti-psychotic, since he deems them worthless. *They need them more than I do,* he tells me. The nurse plays along in the loud, over-patient voice I've come to dread, because it means he's not getting better. *Meet my future wife,* he says, as she has the gall to blush. More fake laughter. I am in the chair in the corner, overly warm in my winter coat, pulled around me like a fortress. I wear ICU delirium like a hairnet. I want to crawl into the bed with my son, hand deliver him to safety like once before.

We'll get through this, I tell him.

Are you still here, he asks, looking up at the ceiling,

singing a Nirvana song under his breath.

Refraction

The way a slant of light can
make the difference between
wanting to sing all the words to
songs you know by heart or
choosing the burial site at random
based on easterly wind currents.
I arrange the chairs in the hospital
room like chess pieces. He calls
out to everyone who passes by
in the hallway. He thinks it is
what he is supposed to do. I bend
my limbs, bite my lip so hard I
draw blood. It's my bodily sacrifice only
it's lost on everyone and he is still
in his membrane of withdrawal. A nurse
fiddles with her loose bun, hanging dejectedly
on the back of her arched neck. She tells me
his withdrawal didn't read the textbook,
meaning: *don't expect miracles.* The floor gives way.
I step over and around her voice
that splinters on the floor like glass.

Defend(ed)

Alienation is a drape made
of brocade. Fancy and smelling like

bad weather. I play peekaboo with my
loneliness. Wear a patch over my weak "I".

If I were the type to wear an apron
mine would be a pattern of wingless

birds, with a sharp, scalloped edge.
You call me: *Mom!* Are you breaking through?

If I squeeze my eyes shut, you are still there, heavy
head to sunken chest. I ask all of the questions

they will not anticipate. They will give me answers they know
know I will not understand, though I try.

I wear my motherhood like a shroud. You, my child,
part the curtain for a glimpse of the other side,

a disinterested point of view.

Limen

How much pressure can
a fragile spine bear?
In the womb, you inherited
a kernel of what some would
call the Truth. All hidden connections
are best, but now we are constellate,
and we have both changed direction.
It was a fetation of various modes
and I was always changing my mind.
I am ready to carry the beaded purse of
blame. I remember when I carried you
that it changed the way I travelled. The ease
with which you announced yourself astounds me
to this day. Like a cantilever from one free-floating
world to the next.

Lupo

We saw the wolf at the door but didn't believe. Oh how he licked and clawed. Our eyes a pentaprism, preserved his behavior. Later, we would remember so much.   Only you could see through his intentions. He both confused and convinced you of the difference between the cure and the kill, the milky film that marked the boundary between want and need.   The wolf flinched with wisdom; traced brain seizures, spasms of the heart, and the tender boredom that breeds intense desire. The salt line through your shirts, the angry rash that snaked arterial routes on your skin, leading the way. The muscles that gave up. The wolf's thick fur will thin in the spring. The barrier between you will grow in proportion to whatever impulse wins in the end. Prayers to the gods it is the right one.

Turn

Shift change.

The nursing student who loves Disney and field hockey (I try to smile) cups a tissue around her mouth, wintergreen piercing the stale air in the room.

She settles into the chair next to his bed as if I weren't there and fiddles with her scorecards. Her only job is to rate his reaction to the brightness of colors, his desire to

drink, the vividness of the stories he might tell. He winces in his sleep and she feigns concern. Then: *I've seen lots of these cases, he'll be fine.* Her soft whisper enrages me.

I heave myself into my heavy winter coat, lick the skin peeling like sheets off my lips. I try to believe in the unseen forces at play. I feel sure that when I leave she will fall asleep

joining my son in his carnivalesque dreams. I walk down the dim and overly heated hallway and wrap the new reality around me, smelling for all the world like sour wine

disguised as mother's milk.

Sartorial

How do you dress for a front
row seat at the suffering of another?
Bring back the days of the lace-edged

perfumed handkerchief to wave in front
of the ones who would be charmed into curing
your syndrome with leftover indulgences

for a family member who might put them to good use.
My memory has a switch: voluntary and involuntary.
Two speeds: farther back and everything is okay now.

In the bed you contemplate your feet and praise that
fact that they are a pair. Your colored coded socks
tell a story that is still a mystery to you. Last week red

meant blood, rage, love and a clenched fist. Today,
yellow for the sun still hiding, the coating on your tongue,
the stains on your sheets, the fear that clings white-knuckled

to everything within your reach. The little rubbery treads on
the bottom are pointless, even to you. *Bought and paid for
and all mine,* you said. In the end, I appreciated the flourish,
nonetheless.

By Now

The doctors should have figured out the
Doctrine of Signatures. Walnuts equal to the brain,
kidney beans to the bean-shaped kidney.
Instead, all of us are hollow-headed

hungry and wondering what day of the week it is.
My sister wears her worried face and
I have to look away. My lady-like grief has betrayed me.
I dab my heavily made up eyes,

garish, in their seemingly callous denial of why I am here.
Today was a good day,
the nurse with the cigarette and coffee breath bellows.
I am silent, questioning

her method of measurement, though admittedly
I am no nursing school graduate. *He's coming back to us,*
she continues as though to shame me
into response. In the meantime, his dinner cools on its tray.

The pudding grows a skin, the chicken puckers while
the cup of winter fruit fairly sings a dirge.
I scrape the tears from my face, head down.

Greet the doctor coming in on my way out.

Ten Facts That Are Pure Truth

1. Falling while under the influence often just looks like clumsiness, not intoxication.
2. Repeating words in a poem is probably okay.
   The reader will adjust.
3. It is risky to say *I love you* to someone who is hallucinating.
4. Strong verbs keep things moving in a poem.
5. The poet is often so tired, and lacks the needed energy to keep going.
6. Explicit blame is pointless. *Pointless.*
7. The alcoholic takes no pleasure in drinking.
8. Crucial facts will reveal themselves like the Second Coming.
9. You will blame yourself.
10. We are all afraid of saying the wrong things. Rebukes are carried on our black breath. *We say them anyway.*

Liminal

Everything you might have
learned before the cock crowed
three times was clearly
a threshold concept.
We had so much to learn.
What did shuddering fear
burn into you that you can
teach others on the line?
That tunnel of darkness goes
on for miles and is filled with the
malignancy of all we can't yet know.
That's where the pain comes from.
One way or another, we will burn.
Hold your breath. Make the sign
of the cross. For your trouble, I will pray
a novena.   With the prayer book in one hand,
I clean the dirt out of my mouth with the other.

The Shape of Things to Come

He uses crypt words and now I dream of all of my sister's
happy endings. The only way to respond to his mysteries
resplendent in the deepest of purples is to invent a few of my
own, apply a logic that for once I can follow. Fire and dying
men, carrion birds and windowsills to lean his elbows on.
There is a twig growing from his ear and he waits for the glue
to put it back, to hold it all together. The sweat pools on his
scalp where his hair has grown thin and I can see my own
third eye reflected in it, crusty, dull, having outlived its
usefulness. *How it failed me. How it failed him.* His hand on
my face, pushing me away. *Pursue, pursue* he trills, a dry
mouth smile as though waiting for an ovation or just the small
pills that will seal him even further away from me and into his
dark-as-midnight membrane.

Anterior Chamber

Someone I loved once gave me a box full of darkness. It took me years to understand that this too, was a gift.
    ---**Mary Oliver**

A day so dark.

I can't tell night   from   day to say nothing of Sunday,
Monday.
Cast iron sky with clouds   *holding*   *holding.*

His eyes unfocused as though encased in a caul
dimming   cornflower blue

          elliptical vaults.

I close the curtains and light the room.
Cold white light   pierces

          like a poison tipped arrow.

I chatter into   the void.
His shaking   hands   covering   his

eyes.   A moan his only

response.

Volta

*Not a cruel song, no, no, not cruel at all. This song
is sweet. It is sweet. The heart dies of this sweetness.*

    ---**Brigit Pegeen Kelly**

The body is not a fortress no matter how hard
we want it to be. I tried to think of a word for it,

but *I am a poet, not a jargoneer.* There are words
I could use, but I'd still be fooling myself.

If my belly is swollen with grief it is because I can't
live one breath to the next, but am expected to.

I wanted to write an entire collection in haiku
all my thoughts truncated, excised of the most

painful parts. Your anti-psychotic syrup
reminds me to focus on the seasons

maybe winter or spring, when things die
or are reborn. There are rules

but we break them all the time. The inside
of the hospital feels like a deserted

airport terminal, everyone either hunched
over something that glows or yoked.

to mechanical life. Your return to the world
will mean I will be Shakespearean in my fear,

my sadness waxing gibbous.
I have nothing but praise for the sympathy

of the well-intentioned, but they've moved on.
Still, I remain, paralyzed in the moment.

I feign optimism but reek of apprehension.
Be kind and forgive me.

Show me the way.

Narratology

> If you desire healing
> let yourself fall ill
> let yourself fall ill.
>   ---Rumi

I wanted to tell a sacred story. I wanted
all the words to run together so you would

have to decode them like a foreign language.
I wanted to feel heat like molten lava,

all certainties eroded, the shine rubbed dull.
And you, in the bionic bed, dank sheets

smelling like a forgotten church for the weak and unforgiving.
and unforgiving. You are like a flickering candle

Crossing an ersatz secular-sacred divide. Cue the doves.
Not dead, just dormant.

Acknowledgements

Heartfelt thanks to so many, but especially my daughter Isabella, my sons Nicholas and Michael, and the Novak's who saw us through, every single step of the way. To my parents, my aunts and uncles, and to Rose Durkin whose friendship and support was rock solid and steadfast. Last but not least, to Jeanne Buckley, as usual, for her wisdom, friendship and care. Thank you to Chad Frame who knows me so well, and knew these poems had to be written and encouraged me.

Thank you, Jon Drucker, for giving these poems a home at West Philly Press.

Thank you, David, for fighting. You are loved more than you know.

Angels in street clothes, every single one of you.

Michelle Reale is the author of seven collections of poetry, including *The Marie Curie Sequence* (Dancing Girl Press, 2017) and *Confini: Poems of Refugees in Sicily* (forthcoming from Cervena Barva Press, 2018), as well as three books on librarianship with a fourth due out in January 2018. Much of her work focuses on Italian-American aspects of memory, narrative and immigration. Her work has been published in many journals both online and in print. She has twice been nominated for a Pushcart Prize. She is an Associate Professor and Librarian at Arcadia University.

Made in the USA
Columbia, SC
12 July 2017